True Life Poetry

by
Dwight Conway

Cork Hill Press
Indianapolis

Cork Hill Press
7520 East 88th Place, Suite 101
Indianapolis, Indiana 46256-1253
1-866-688-BOOK
www.corkhillpress.com

Copyright © 2003 by Dwight Conway

All rights reserved under International and Pan-American Copyright Conventions. With the exception of brief quotations in critical reviews or articles, no part of this work may be reproduced or transmitted in any form or by any means, electronic or mechanical, including photocopying, recording, or any information storage or retrieval system, without permission in writing from the publisher.

Trade Paperback Edition: 1-59408-163-8

Printed in the United States of America

1 3 5 7 9 10 8 6 4 2

STATES SURROUNDED BY WATER

Hawaii is the place everyone should go
Not too much of Hawaii many people know
It has very many beautiful scenes of water
You can rest near a lake for hours and a quarter
Everyone go look at the state surrounded by water
At wonderful sights of Hawaii
That would look good show nuff it would

Everyone should speak less than they do
Many times they're speaking, they should listen to you
Never speak what you think; speak what you know
A misunderstanding could knock you to and fro
One thing everyone could pay is attention
And to do that you would surely have to listen
Best to be understood and you really could

Last time it was raining a guy took sick
And his job lie had to quit
Stayed in the hospital for a half of a year
And his family was full of tear
Next time it rained, his son was going out
And his mother said you don't know what it's all about
Put on your hood because you should

THE OCEANS

The largest ocean is the Pacific
Takes over thirty percent of the earth
If you cross it be specific
You'll get your money's worth

Atlantic is second in size
And has the most business
From overseas cities be making buys
New York City is a witness

Running into the Atlantic Ocean
Is the Indian down south
It's the third largest portion
Joining the Atlantic's mouth

Antarctic is an ocean in itself
Define zone in the south of the largest three
Many humans and mammals been put to death
When the winter freezes the sea

You could make the Arctic host
Although it's the smallest ocean
There you will find whales most
And seals in large portions

There's more water than land
More than seventy percent
Each portion is used for traveling
And separating the continents

THE STATE OF FLORIDA

The state of Florida is the southernmost state
With a very large population
Sometimes people just can't wait
To get to the warmest, state of the nation

Florida is a place where many people like to go
Because the weather stays warm enough to reach
Enough people who were out in the cold
And sent to Miami Beach

The nickname of this state is Sunshine
The state motto is "In God We Trust"
The state of Florida is just so fine
Because the people keep peace and just

Sabal Palm is the state tree
The state flower is the Orange Blossom
Some roads have Palm Trees all the way — Gee!
The fun leaves when you've lost em

The state bird is Mockingbird
That we should all know
I can give you all my word
That Florida is where you want to go.

COLORADO

It's a pleasure to look at a beautiful scene
Trees from side to side covered with green
With big mountains covered with snow
Sometimes high, sometimes low

Near the bottom of the scene is a bridge of frame
That people cross on the side lane
With orange rocks beneath
And maybe wild animals with sharp teeth

You have a river at the bottom so clean
If you've seen the Colorado River, you know what I mean
There are a few clouds in the sky
Telling you that bad weather is high

A small chapel sits in the scene alone
Behind some trees where most of them are gone
If there's ever been a scene for you to see
This is a beautiful one for you and me

CITY OF LIGHT

We should want to take a glance
At the capital of the country of France
Large in population, but small in size
You won't believe the scenery of your eyes

Go do your shopping at Sanger-Harris
And then you'll be on your way to Paris
The city with lots of power
The tallest structure is the Eiffel Tower

The nickname of Paris is the City of Light
Looks mighty beautiful day and night
Many famous Cathedrals still standing
Like Notre Dame, built over and over again

And I am sure some day
You will be on your way
To take a look at the City of Lights
Where you'll find everything so bright.

THE GRAND CANYON

Everyone should go to see the Grand Canyon
And take your boys and girls
It's over a mile-deep-sculptured gorge
Among the natural wonders of the world

217 miles long, 4 to 8 miles wide
And more than one mile deep
It lies several thousand feet above sea level
The canyon cuts very deep

It is something for you to take a picture of it
Because it is very neat
With towering buttes, mesas and valleys
Just right for the eyes to feast

And if you are going to take pictures of it
You've got to take more than one
In order to get the whole canyon
And see what all's been done

One thing for sure, in the summertime
The canyon becomes very hot
But yet and still it's still a thrill
Arizona's got something we ain't got

THE MIDDLE ATLANTIC STATES

There are three Middle Atlantic States
Belonging to the nation
Each one of these states alone
Has a very large population

New Jersey is the smallest one
But has very large crowds
Large cities take nearly half
And the people very proud

Pennsylvania comes next
With undefeated Superbowl Champs
Happens to be the state of steel
Where it stays foggy and damp

Last and least, the state of New York
Which is the empire over all
Has cities with many skyscrapers
Some over a thousand feet tall

THE BIG APPLE

New York, chief city of the United States
Twenty-four hours daily, keeps open its gates
It is divided into five parts
To find your way around, you'll have to know the chart

Brooklyn is the largest in population
More people except three cities of the nation
Has many neighborhoods, at least twenty-eight
Heavy numbers of people, enough to find you a mate

Queens is the largest one in size
Go there and you will find a big surprise
Queens is another large residential section
Be careful up there, or you'll lose connection

Bronx has a real nice large zoo
Cute little monkeys and wild animals, too
Bronx is famous for many parks and boulevards
Follow directions on the highways, it won't be so hard

In size, Manhattan is the smallest one
And will surprise you that alone
Has half the land taken up for business
And the other half, a million and a half people, I'm a
	witness

That leaves one more, Staten Island, the smallest one
With less people, and not many more to come
They're not looking for them anyway
They're now as large as they want to be today

MAE QUEEN

I once lived in New Orleans
Met a young lady named Mae King
I would call her Mae Queen
Because she was the prettiest human being

For her, deep in my heart I had love
That was sent to me from above
Everything was white as a dove
I would never use a sub

In Christianity, she was very strong
I loved to hear her sing a song
Our togetherness didn't take long
We never treated each other wrong

Once we settled by the lake
Myself and Mae, my mate
First thing you know we both ate
Second thing you know we were on a date

I said to her "I love you"
She said back "I love you, too"
I told her, that I knew
As we both kissed and left at two

BUSIEST SEAPORT

New York is the country's largest city
For its size, it is very pretty
You will find so much to see
A lot you couldn't believe to be

This is the world's largest seaport
Using water traffic of all types of sort
Many things are brought to New York from overseas
And spread around the country to the majorities

Brooklyn has the largest population
More than all but three cities of the nation
Has at least 28 geographical neighborhoods
And receives great value from producing goods

Bronx is another one, not near as large
But is heavily populated by means of charge
Happens to have a mighty large zoo
Long island, Crotona Park, and Van Cortland, too

Queens is the biggest borough in size
On the southwest of Manhattan it lies
There are buildings over three hundred years old
They are keeping them for landmarks to uphold

Manhattan Island is the busiest place
The city has among the space
At one end you'll see New York downtown
At the other end you'll see residents, some underground

Staten Island is the only one downtown doesn't connect
But many go to Manhattan Island to collect
They have many different kinds of transportation
To get to the downtown population

DIFFERENT WAYS OF TRAVELING

Once upon a time I went on a tour
And one thing that I was very sure
I traveled many ways I didn't expect
And everyone showed their honest respect

Now this trip was mighty far
Everything started in my brother's car
He took me to D.F.W. Airport
And that's where I began to board

All the way to London on a plane
And then to Dover on a train
We came to the end of Dover, the very tip
And crossed the English Channel on a ship

Next thing you know we were on a bus
Happy as can be with peace and just
And believe me, we had a good time
Visiting other cities, the foreign kind

Finally, the tour came to an end
No more time we had to spend
The traveling went backwards from before
Ended when I got home and shut the door

TRAVELING ON THE WATER

We were sailing across the water
Looked out about every quarter
Saw nothing but waves
That were moving so brave
I had with me my wife and daughter

While we were moving on the ship
We thought it was a nice trip
By water it took longer
But we didn't hunger
Stayed moving till we got to the tip

We saw other ships go by
We looked up to see planes fly
We were traveling very smooth
Felt comfortable as we moved
End of trip was drawing nigh

The trip came to an end
No more time we had to spend
We enjoyed it so much
We didn't get enough
So we started on another one then

LOVE AT FIRST SIGHT

I was going on a trip on vacation
To see other parts of the nation
Where cities had beautiful decorations
Met a beautiful young lady

We both conversated sitting down
There were no chairs, so we sat on the ground
Love is what I was sure I had found
In the year 1980

After camp we went home
Then we talked on the telephone
We conversed very long
This was my new Mrs. Daley

I could see it from above
I knew that I had found love
My heart flew as high as a dove
All over I felt kind of shaky

THE OPEN HEART

I once took a trip overseas
And met a young lady named Hazel Keys
We both had to pay touring fees
When we were ready to start

We both traveled on the same bus
In the Lord's name we did trust
We stayed with our tour like we must
And pretty well played our parts

I sec we were from the same state
And on the same tour, Cosmos 8
She and I would conversate
Together in a nice sort

She once gave me a big surprise
Hard to believe with my own eyes
Visiting with me very wise
At my church and that was sharp

Said sweet things about me that day
That anyone could ever say
Sung a beautiful solo and did stay
Her voice was sharper than a dart

I felt so enthused to see her there
Felt real good everywhere
Everything was good, bright and fair
And really gave me a clean heart

I hope we meet each other again
Before the Lord takes us in
Next time we'll have more to spend
On a very different passport

CAMPING THROUGH THE NIGHT

There was a man who had a son
Trying to find somewhere to camp
They had plenty of food, blankets and water
And also a battery lamp

The son went and chopped up some wood
To build a camping fire
So they could stay warm through the night
And continue to go higher

The father cooked a real nice supper
Some mashed potatoes and steak
And for dessert they both had
A piece of German chocolate cake

So after dinner conversated together
And then they fell asleep
And woke up early the next morning
With nothing for them to weep

The next morning the son cooked breakfast
Some sausages and fried eggs
And then they were on their way
To do what they had pledged

SIGHTSEEING

Beside the Mississippi, in the city of Saint Louis
You will find the Gateway Arch
In the right hand of the Statue of Liberty
You will see a lighted torch

Right at the edge of Downtown Dallas
You will see the Reunion Tower
In San Francisco, you'll see the Golden Gate
You may want to rest on it an hour

Headed west you can also find
Where you can stand in four states
You will be near the Mile High City
Where many people just can't wait

If you want temperature where you can stay warm
Then go deep south to Florida
You won't be too far from the Peach Tree Plaza
Located in Atlanta, Georgia

EATING PLACES NEARBY

I can walk to food places any time
And buy food for my body to go incline
Although I don't have a car
And I don't have to go too far

I'm one block from Minyard's Grocery Store
When I'm hungry and need to eat
Instead of driving a car to go
I can always use my feet

I'm a few blocks away from Hardemans Barbeque
Who has the best beef and ribs for you
There's no cooking for you to do
You'll get the best potato salad too

The main place to keep you out of the kitchen
Is where I worked at for several years
That could be none other than Church's Fried Chicken
That you can eat without tears

You don't necessarily need a dish
To get everything you wish
Get some Harrell Fried Fish
And that should complete your day

CREPE MYRTLE TREES

Crepe Myrtle Trees are so pretty
Grow at least fifteen feet tall
Makes your yard look good in the city
During the summer and fall

During these two seasons they have beautiful roses
Sometimes red, sometimes white
Near the end of the fall, the scene closes
On a nice cool autumn night

These trees look very pretty
When they're standing in pairs
You want to feel no one's giving you pity
From these roses they bear

This happens not to be a rosebush
'Cause you're looking at many more
You'll really think you've been pushed
When you first open the door

You can pick some off the tree when they bloom
All are about the same size
They will make a good decoration for your room
You won't believe your eyes

GOOD DEAL THAT WAS REAL

We were on a penny shortage a little while back
All business places needed as many as would make a pack
I would put them in rolls when I was home and sat
And would take them to Burger King, now what you think
    of that

The manager would see to me getting a free meal
In front of everybody, I wouldn't have to conceal
To me that was a very nice deal
May sound like a joke, but believe me it was real

Sometimes I would get a double meat with cheese
And a strawberry malt and was never teased
Along with fries, I was well pleased
It felt like someone was giving me a trip overseas

As you know all managers aren't fair
Sometimes your load is a little heavier to bear
It all depends on who is there
For me to get more than a breath in the air

HOW TO MAKE AND SAVE MONEY

A good way to make and save money is going out
    collecting cans
At the same time you pick them up, squeeze them with
    your hands
If they're too filthy to squeeze, stomp them with your feet
And never put anything extra in bags, never try and cheat

Going to sets of apartments, you will find all you need
Always make your route alone, always on your feet
You won't only find cans, but you'll also find cash
You can't find it in a car, all of it you'll pass

You'll walk upon soda water bottles, now and then a case
Before you get home you can sell them by passing the
    right place
$1.60 for a case, some bottles 20 cents, some a dime
You'll find out it does add up with you every time

If you get paid on Fridays and it's time for another pay
Bank just about the whole check and sell cans the next day
You might get $50.00 or more but even if not that much
You'll get enough to start again and that gives you the real
    touch

When you're ready to go on a trip, go and get travelers
    checks
The only cash you'll have is from the cans you have
    fetched
It will be several days before the first check is broken
And you will feel like you have received a very large token

A FINE MEAL

There was a bear walking through the woods
Looking for him some daily foods
Wasn't as easy as he thought it should
But he was doing his best

He saw a squirrel beside a tree
And said to himself, "You're for me"
He charged him hard as can be
And on his back fell a hornet's nest

He was being stung all around
It made him fall to the ground
He made very loud sounds
But that was no success

For a long time the bear was hurt
Trying to cool off in the dirt
He couldn't hardly do any work
They had to give him some test

He decided not to try and make another attack
On a squirrel 'cause of what happened to his back
Since this was truly a serious fact
The bear was real blest

DO YOU LOVE PENNIES

Everyone wants a dollar
No one wants pennies
Not even if it equals
The sum of very many

If you don't want the penny
You can't have the dollar
They'll both stay with me
No matter how you holler

I have here with me
One hundred dollars worth
To give away to you
On your anniversary, the first

I'm giving you what I can
It's best you take them
You will feel so good
And want to sing a hymn

I don't have rubies
I don't have gold
I do have pennies
I hope you can hold

INTERNAL REVENUE SERVICE

The man with the largest family on earth
Is the one who really gets his money's worth
Had kinfolks ever since the first birth
And you're kin to him like I am

He didn't do any work direct
Just sits on the sideline and collects
Makes it possible for things to be erect
Taking it easy as a little lamb

Never in this history has this man gone broke
Could be because he deals with many folks
He's never cheated any one, never tried to joke
And has never been in a jam

The money he collects is called tax
What makes you feel good is getting some back
When you have to pay you don't feel relaxed
And it messes up your day with a ham

This man could have more people than the Lord
Because everybody pays taxes on one accord
You won't receive from him any kind of reward
And if you were looking for one, I'm sorry man

He hasn't got any sisters or brothers
He hasn't got any fathers and mothers
Four billion people in his family, soon be others
The man I'm speaking about is Uncle Sam

CRIME DOESN'T PAY

Once there was an Indian who had a beautiful horse
That was very intelligent and very well trained, of course

The Indian's name was Chief White Wolf, leader of the tribe
Made visits to others when there was something to be
 described

He kept his tribe busy by making clothes and pearls
And sent them to be sold to different parts of the world

Next thing you know they were very rich
Had more money than anyone could ever wish

There was a little boy who was so bad
Wanted everything the Indians had

 He would always come in the middle of the night
And would get the horses out of sight

That would be so there wouldn't be any noise
And he would get what he wanted for the other boys

He tried to steal a horse, the one they called "Pint"
Said "I shall return" and sooner than you think.

White Wolf whistled for his horse to toss him to the ground
And when the horse did, the boy made a loud sound
As he got off the ground, he was badly hurt
And so embarrassed for the horse to throw him into the
 dirt

He decided to leave them alone when he found out that
 crimes do not pay
And became friends with the Indians and decided to stay

PERFECT NUMBER

This is poem number sixty-six
A very significant number
That is heard very much
And more than what I wonder

The average height of a man
Is usually six feet tall
He may grow six inches more
Or he may not grow any more at all

As you know the bible
Has exactly sixty-six books
The smallest library in the world
You can tell by its looks

A good understanding
Can clear what needs to be fixed
For the number of man
Is six hundred threescore and six

BROTHERS

Once there were two brothers that lived in Ohio
One thought he was tougher than the other
Every day he would tease the one who was chicken
And he would always go and tell Mother

Willie was the one who thought he was bad
He went and urged up another fight
Put scars all over the face of Billy
His face stayed swollen the whole night

It just so happens Willie went too far
Billy once showed he was tough, too
Willie came and gave Billy a sock on the head
Billy said "I'm saying this to you"

I don't want you to come and do that again
I don't want you to even come about
What are you going to do if I come again
Come on and try it and you'll find out

Willie came once more to give him a sock
Billy ducked and gave him one in the nose
And there came blood pouring down from his face
Same color as a beautiful red rose

WINTER

I once saw a man fall
Who was very very tall
He had to make a phone call
But couldn't get on his feet

It was sixteen (16) degrees
The man caught cold and began to sneeze
Suddenly, there came a stronger breeze
The man prayed for heat

Slowly, he got up off the ground
Suddenly, he heard a sound
And immediately turned around
And there came driving in the sleet

A stranger who asked if he wanted a ride
If so, get in on the other side
Where are you going in this weather so tired
Just trying to get off the street

BECOMING A DALLAS POLICE OFFICER

In order to become a Police of Dallas
You must be at least 19
You will be sent to the City Hall palace
To have a talk with the Dean

You must have a little College
Enough for 45 hours
Before you be accepted to the force
To have the police power

You must take the physical test
And promise you'll do your best
And when you take the polygraph test
Your action will show the rest

You can be done received traffic tickets
To become a Dallas City Cop
But you can't have no felonies convicted
Or we'll put in your hands a mop

You will be searched for background investigation
And if cleared, you'll be assigned a station
At the best department in the nation
The Dallas Police Department

BECOMING A DEPUTY SHERIFF

In order to become a Deputy Sheriff
You must be done finished high school
You must be 21 or over
And work by the rule

You must have 14 weeks of Academy
And not be easily played a fool
And don't try to play others crazy
Just sit down and play it cool

Three times a year you must get supplies
And hop back on your mule
To go to the firing range for practice
And try to shoot bottles off a stool

On your day off why not go to the hall
And shoot a game of pool
And if you think that you're so good
Shoot for a package of Kool

BECOMING A PARK POLICEMAN

To become a park police you need 45 hours of College
Because they want all officers to have knowledge
We want you to be in good physical health
Your starting salary would be a good wealth

These college hours do mean a lots
With more than 45 you're on the right spot
You must be 21 or older in age
To have the authority to put someone in a cage

You must be a nice guy or gal
And can't have favoritism with your pal
You must be tough, have courage, and good looking
And don't worry too much about what's cooking

You must be suave, a lady's man, and brave
To lock up other officers in a cave
As said earlier, no favoritism on the spot
Be able to arrest your ma, whether you like it or not

THE CLEANING CREW

Once there was a crew
Who was stripping a floor
Behind the buff machine
Louis stand

Lennis was picking up
And was doing it so sloppy
Putting pressure on Alton, the rinser
Who was giving him a helping hand

As everyone was looking
And saw it was poor rinsing
The rinse man said
I'm doing the best I can

The one on the buff said
You can do better than that
Why don't you rinse right
That I know you can do better than

And Alfred said
Alton ain't rinsing
Alton's picking up
Behind the pick up man

COME AND GET IT

Once there was a family of four,
The head of the family was Mr. Moore
He stayed busy with many chores.
Out of all the work he led,
Because he was the head

He had a wife who was thirty-one.
Burt and Bart were their two sons.
Both of them were sort of young—
Both slept in the same bed
One at the foot, one at the head

Early Thanksgiving morning, Mr. Moore and Burt
Went out in the yard to work
His brother Bart had been hurt
So he stayed in with Peg
Got him a book and read

Suddenly, the Thanksgiving dinner was done
Mrs. Moore asked everyone to come
They continued doing what they had begun
Got tired and wanted to go to bed

Bart showed up and saw his mother mad
An idea came to him to make her glad
"Mother, since they're acting bad
When I get out there ask again," he said.
"And they'll be in as fast as lead."

Bart went out with the others
And then he heard a voice from his mother
Saying, "Bart are you coming, your father, and brother?"
"Yes, Mam, first come, first fed
Last one's a rotten egg."

So they all took off and began to run
As though they were having lots of fun
And there they were all to mom
"Thank you, Bart, and you may be fed"
"So you tricked us Bart and made us soreheads"

WHAT'S GOOD FOR A COLD DAY

One morning out in the chill
I was standing on top of a hill
It began to rain
Took a long time to drain
It was amazing I didn't become ill

I started running down
I fell to the flat ground
I saw an old shack
And went to the back
And never did hear a sound

After a while the storm went by
I stayed there to let it dry
Next morning I went back up
And took my little pup
And heard birds sing as they flew high

They put on my face a smile
They kept us company for a while
As the songs were being heard
By the cute little birds
You could hear them from a mile

THE POOL GAME

Come on Henry, play it cool
Rack 'em up, I'll shoot you a game of pool
Get the cue so we can choose
Makes no difference, you're going to lose

Since I won the choosing, I'll break
You better be successful and make no mistakes
Because the very first time you miss
I'm going to put on you some real English

Well did anything fall
You made one big ball
With big balls I'll know I'll win
I bet you won't play me again

This is my favorite also, the low
You won't get a shot any more
That tells me something's out of line
Because now I know somebody's lying

I'll shoot the eight ball in the side
And let the cue ball be my guide
Oh No! I lost this match!
I hit it a little too hard and scratched

B M A SYSTEMS

Have you ever heard of a company named B M A systems
Just in case you haven't then sit down and listen

This company is run by Mr. Samuel Brown
He has what you want; it would be hard to turn down

He has all kinds of alarms for homes and also cars
You'll find out for yourself that alarms are better than bars

You can feel more comfortable when you have a real
    alarm
You can sleep at night and won't have to be armed

While you're at work have it on 'cause you care
I assure when you get home everything will be there

You will have a private number that no one could use but
    you
And if you don't know it, they'll come after you, too.

Burglars can easier be caught when you have the silent
    one
But sometimes you may forget that you have this alarm on

An alarm will also show you how fast a burglar can run
And if you get to see him it will be lots of fun

THE CATCH

During the World Series
In the year of 1954
An outstanding play happened
That you think won't happen any more

With a runner already on third base
Viv Wertz hit a long drive to deep center
Willie Mays running with his back to the plate
Made the catch and the runner could not enter

It's hard to believe he made the catch
On this very outstanding play
It's also hard to believe
That he could throw the ball all the way

This truly helped the Giants
Defeat the Indians in the first game
And it also gave Willie Mays
A very popular name

He made a double play
Out of what should have been a double
Either he had a very strong arm
Or the runner with his legs had trouble

CHAMPIONS OF '83

If you make the play-offs good for you
But you don't know what we're going to do
We'll kick everyone out and go the Super Bowl
It's just like receiving a truck of gold

We did it before, and we can do it again
We are the best, the Washington Redskins
We happen to be the ones who own this land
That's why we keep the Super Bowl in our hands

We won't lie about it; we have hard times
When we do, we make Indian hats out of dimes
You've heard the saying "Action is louder than words"
You must shoot straight in order to shoot birds

There's no team sitting out there we'll dodge
We'll send you home sad enough to sleep in your garage
So everyone hear me from north, south, east, and west
When you speak of the Redskins, you're speaking of the
    best

OUTSTANDING WILLIE MAYS

Once upon a time in earlier days
Was a baseball player named Willie Mays
People would love to give him praise
Because Willie would make outstanding plays

No matter how far you hit the ball
Willie would always get the call
He would not let it fall
He made some catches against the wall

People on base knew they'd better stay
Because Willie could throw the ball all the way
Willie could always make the play
If you tried to run, you would pay

Fairfield, Alabama was Willie's home
After the game he would talk on the phone
He could make the ball sound like stone
He once hit the top of the Astrodome

He was also furious at the plate
It seems he never swung too late
People would pay money at the gate
To see Willie knock the ball out of state

WINNER OF TODAY

I know a man filled with action
Speaking of none other than Reggie Jackson
Won two World Series for Oakland A's
By making some very outstanding plays

And for the Yankees, won two
That proves he did what he's suppose to do
Once played for Baltimore, they didn't keep him
When they saw him with the Yankees, they started
    weeping

Got Martin fired from the Yankees
Because they had a fight on TV
Another World Series he won was for Lemon, Bob
Had the other team feeling like they've been robbed

Mr. October was his nickname
One day he'll be in the Hall of Fame
It will be an honour as fun
He was the only one to hit back-to-back runs (In World
    Series)

EASTER

I was looking up early one morning
Listening to some birds in a tree sing
All trees were beautiful with leaves green
Everything was a wonderful scene

I decided to sit outside a few hours this day
Seeing children come out and play
Everything we saw was God's creations
We were really enjoying our recreation

One thing we saw that was very funny
Hopping in our house was a little gray bunny
That reminded us before we got away
It was Happy Easter Day

LABOR DAY

A time to visit a family member
It is the first Monday in September
This happens to be Labor Day
A time to watch your children play

You can also have a family picnic
And invite neighbors to come and to sit
Having plenty of food to be served
And plenty of music to be heard

Refreshments and beer, the quicker you run out
Everyone will be ready to go about
They will remember for a long time
What happened in month number nine

Playing different games will be fun
That will make more people come
The more come, the longer it will last
And no one will be ready to go home fast

When it's all over, something you should know
In case you are looking to clean up slow
You will also have your closest neighbor
Standing there to help you labor

And you two working together as brothers
After you say "Goodbye" to others
He'll help you like a gentleman, there's no doubt
If he don't, kick his hind out.

THANKSGIVING

It all started in the fall
When we had a house full of guests
And had contacted them by a telephone call
And told them to come visit us out west

And boy didn't we have a big dinner
Turkey, yams, salad, rolls, and dressing
1 know that was truly a winner
And a Happy Thanksgiving Day

The food was ready when they showed up
And they were ready to start on it, too
We also had a little pup
Who wasn't going to be left out, I knew

My wife fixed everybody's plate
And didn't leave out a thing
You know I just couldn't wait
To get a piece of turkey wing

After dinner, our guests had to leave
One thing we had to say
We'll come to see you on Christmas Eve
And stay till New Year's Day

DR. MARTIN LUTHER KING, JR.

Once there was a man named Martin Luther King
Who once had a wonderful, wonderful dream
Although one day, the dream did come true
And for that to happen, this is what we had to do
Since the whole country was so segregated
It changed, and everyone became integrated
Not only on jobs but everywhere you go
People quit being so quick to say "no"
Man got many innocent people in jail
But God won't send innocent people to hell
Martin Luther King was put under arrest
For being out on the streets at his best
King began his leadership of civil rights
After a Negro woman refused to give her seat to a white
After being arrested she and Martin Luther King
Got together with blacks and changed everything
That struck attention to all supervisors
One thing in every town they said to bus drivers
Get behind that wheel, collect that fare, and get those keys
And let those people sit anywhere they please

Still the whites didn't want to cooperate with blacks
So they thought maybe they would make some attacks
By sicking their dogs on them for a good bite
Or their water hose to get a shower before night
One year Martin Luther King became co-pastor
Of his father's church to do more work for the Master
His father's church was located in the city of Atlanta
And he became pastor in the State of Alabama
He founded the Southern Christian Leadership Conference which features
An organization of civil rights to give to Negro preachers
This also hit another great big keynote
To give the black people the legal right to vote
In April of '68 in Memphis, Tennessee
He was preparing a march and many were with thee
After bringing the black man from a mighty long way
He was assassinated by James Earl Ray

WHICH IS BEST

Which is best, Christmas or Easter Day
Many people would say neither one
The reason that would be what they would say
Is because they're so scared to be wrong
I have a very important reason
For saying the best is his birth
Not because of what you receive that season
Only because of what it's worth
Although Easter season, when on the cross
Is what saved us from sin
It also helped you find the lost
With his death, we did win
But the reason why Christmas is best
I'll tell you as you blow your horn
He never would have been laid to rest
If he hadn't ever been born

A BEAUTIFUL SIGHT

I want to tell you about Colorado State
That's been beautiful since 1928
If you want to visit, it's never too late
To see some outstanding sights, you won't have to wait
Evergreen trees from left to right
Up in the day makes a beautiful sight
Especially when the sun shines on them so bright
Although, there isn't much to see at night
Another thing you will see so clean
Is a very large huge size stream
Looks a lot better in the spring
Many people camp beside it and sing
Colorful rocks are in the scene, also
Very high mountains covered with snow
A frame bridge you will find below
Across it, everyday the people go
Out of all states, this one looks best
Because its sights are better than the rest
Every year it has plenty of guest
From ones which take their vacation out west

THE DEMOCRATIC PARTY OF THE 20TH CENTURY

Woodrow Wilson was the first Democrat
Who won in 1912
Served eight long years as president
Next was Franklin Roosevelt
Roosevelt was chosen as one of the greatest
That we've had in the latest
Years because he was one of the straightest
Presidents we've ever had
Harry Truman was next in line
Took over after Roosevelt fell
To be sure he was understood fine
His main words were damn and hell
Kennedy was getting good praise
Whatever he said, it stays
Although he traveled the wrong ways
His assassination ended his days
Lyndon Baines Johnson took over
Because he was the vice
These men are all among the greatest
Because they were all nice

WARS

As long as there will be an earth
There will also be war
From now until the last birth
Sometimes near, sometimes far
You see bombs drop from planes
To blow up a number of ships
If it falls into the right lane
Everyone on board will be dipped
There are many things which causes them
Jealousy and greediness are two
The country shows the men films
To give an idea what to do
Before anyone begins to fight
They should try and hold it down
If not, then they should show their might
And blow up the whole town
Although, we better show peace
Or in the plane we'll be flown up
And before it has a chance to cease
It will truly be blown up

MISSOURI

Starts with an M
Ends with an I
Sets near the center
With eight neighbors close by
Illinois on the right
Left has Kansas power
Arkansas at the bottom
And at the top is Iowa
Bottom left is Oklahoma
Bottom right is Tennessee
Top left is Nebraska
And bottom right is Kentucky

STATUE OF LIBERTY

Out in the water of New York City
Standing very high, looking so pretty
The Statue of Liberty stands out in the shore
On a pedestal that's 154
Upon her head you'll see a spiked crown
A torch in her right hand that never comes down
The broken chains are at her feet
People from everywhere go to meet
The statue wear robes of different kinds
In her left hand the Tablet of Law you'll find
From Empire State Building, it looks like a little woman
See the difference when you go out there to stand
Thinking about the statue gives you a lift
To the United States this was a big gift
Long as you live freedom you'll get
And one thing to remember, keep the torch lit

COMMANDER IN CHIEFS OF AMERICA

One reason why Lincoln was so brave
Cause he had nerve to free the slaves
Most historians call Lincoln the strongest
Although Franklin Roosevelt was in the longest
Grover Cleveland won two nonconsecutive terms
Lost one, but that proves he was still concerned
Coolidge put us in depression; we stayed there under Hoover
And Roosevelt made things a whole lot smoother
More presidents were from Virginia, the total of eight
Four of the first five were from this state
The last from Virginia was Woodrow Wilson
The Commander In Chief during World War I
The one who really had a load to carry
Was the Missouri Man, Truman, Old Harry
Some you can say plenty about, some you can't
There's not much to say on Ulysses S. Grant
Last to die in office was Kennedy, John Fitzgerald
That covered many pages in The Dallas Times Herald
Many people in the 80's were doing lots of begging
Cause they lost their job under the leadership of Reagan

THE RIFLEMAN

Out on nine acres of land
Lived someone called The Rifleman
And surely his name
Was Lucas McCain
Who could hit any target you plan
Mark McCain, his son
Helped get the chores done
And it was a battle
To keep up the cattle
Believe me, they weren't having fun
His rifle had a part to play
On things McCain couldn't say
Was always on hand
For criminals and
When they tried something, they'd pay
They lived there for a long time
On acres, the total of nine
They kept it forever
Decided to sell never
Talking about it, wasn't worth a dime
We'll never forget this man
Worked out many things he planned
People stayed out of his way
Cause this man didn't play
Better known as The Rifleman

A BIG UPSET

During the football season of 83
Dallas did a big favor for me
Had been to the playoffs more than any of thee
Felt they were at the top of the deck
But you must remember to get the job done
You can't take it easy on anyone
You may know that a large sum
Of money people lost with bets
You were hearing the wrong kind of noise
From the fans of the Dallas Cowboys
The Buffalo Bills were filled with joys
And hollered out "a big upset" "a big upset"!
As you remember, this one game
Was Buffalos' only win with aim
Dallas did not look the same
Because they were filled with sweat
This year the playoff hopes they missed
And it was all cause of this
They said Next time there'll be no risk
Cause this game we'll never forget

UNBELIEVABLE MIRACLE

One Saturday, I was getting cans out of a dumpster
That equaled to a very large summer
I got from this dumpster a little over twenty
As you know that isn't near plenty
After splitting the bag opened, cans I found
And that's when I started tossing them to the ground
This dumpster was at a beauty shop
They don't drink beer, but lots of pop
To find out there were cans in the bag
I hit it on the side and heard them in the trash
It helped me get my bag more filled
And my pocket with a twenty-dollar bill
This was really hard to believe
But it wasn't hard for me to receive
Whoever put it in there, I want to say thanks
I paid my phone bill without going to the bank

THE VEGETABLE MAN

In the spring, as the weather was getting warmer
On twelve acres of land lived a farmer
A mile down the road lived his mother
Along with her, lived his older brother
The farmer would always ride into town
And get plenty supplies when prices were down
He would shop for himself, mother, and brother
Everything he got, he shared with the others
His brother grew a large vegetable garden
Got milk from cows and put it in cartons
He would go to his garden and pick some tomatoes
Bring them in the house along with sweet potatoes
From one of the cows, they would have some steak
And what a very nice meal they ate
The three sat at the table and had dinner
After which, straight up to bed they entered

OUT IN THE COLD

One good thing for a nice cold day
Is birds flying from every which way
You can rest back and hear them sing
You can also see them wave their wings
Birds have some good warm feathers
That's what make them enjoy cold weather
Although, we mostly be inside
Trying to keep warm our hides
What's for some is not for all
We enjoy weather till end of fall
Everything stays warm except hands and toes
That's because you have over your body more clothes

WHAT KEEPS THE BUS DRIVER AWAKE

Driving sleepy, there's a lot of danger
More than meeting with an unknown stranger
Some buses continue to drive all night long
Never stop unless there's something to go wrong

If passengers go asleep, that's okay
Long as awake the driver can stay
He has to think of something while he drives
For safety to keep his passengers alive

Every minute through the night, high he flips
His headlights then he closes back the lips
He continues if nothing's on the road but the bus
Because in himself he do not trust

Five seconds of sleep will get you out of line
And cause the lives of more than twenty-nine
One way he keeps himself awake through the nights
Is relaxing while driving and playing with the lights

ANNUAL CHOIR DAY

This time I would like to
Say to everyone here
We're very happy to see you here
Filled with lots of love and cheer
Whatever you do please feel free
Anyone don't like it you send them to me
We are all friends
Glad to see you back
To hear Rev. Webb preach once more
Touch every heart like he did before
Cause he can get it going and make the choir sing
If you heard him before, you know what I mean

From Giggs Chapel you came today
Visit us on 26th of May
This day comes once a year I reckon
That's why I say you're welcome...welcome...welcome

YOU'LL NEVER HAVE TOO MANY

The first thing you should do is set you up a goal
If you reach it, you will be at top of the pole
Never let a can pass you whether it's new or old
If it's aluminum pick it up whether it's half or whole
Make a straight line by the curve or upon the lot
Then drive your truck over them; it'll crush all you've got
If you're a very good aimer, you'll hit the jackpot
But still you have to place the cans in the right spot
In a short time you'll be done crushed them all
Then you'll be ready to take them to the Aluminum Hall
Then with the money you've made, you can have a ball
Don't forget what crushed them, The Automatic Machine
         it's called
Every time you pick up a can, you're picking up a penny
Going to the right place, you'll see a sum of plenty
Always remember that you're to never come back with any
But the main thing to remember is You'll Never Have Too
         Many

SPRINGTIME

I stepped out on my porch one day
And there was plenty I could say
As I was looking each and every way
Everything was beautiful and children out to play
People were out in their yards planting flowers
And spent out there a number of hours
Everyone worked with different powers
Some of the trees looked like tall towers
Although the trees were very green
And the flowers was a wonderful scene
It was a pleasure to hear the birds sing
This was truly the first day of spring

PETER'S DENIAL

Into the palace, they brought in
Peter, one of the Masters' strongest men
And began to ask him if he knew the Lord
They remembered he was the one fighting with the sword
He answered and said "the man he didn't know"
And immediately the cock did crow
They asked him again and he said "Not I"
That was because he didn't want to die
After a while, they asked him again
And quickly he said he didn't know the man
The people knew that the statement wasn't true
That's why for the second time the cock crew
And Peter remembered the word of Christ
That before the cock shall crow twice
First ye shall deny me thrice
He wept bitterly and that wasn't nice

BONANZA

Late one evening, getting close to night
Men came to Virginia City, named Cartwright
A very big piece of land they bought
With a very big amount of money they brought
We ask you all to step a little closer
And take a better look at the Ponderosa
Owned by Ben Cartwright and his sons
Each and everyday they're busy ones
They're so busy taking care of cattle
That's why they haven't got time to tattle
The Ponderosa is a big piece of land
The Cartwrights can always use an extra hand
Hoss seems to be more busy at the table
While Adam stays pretty busy at the stable
Little Joe is always on the road somewhere
While Ben is keeping up the Ponderosa with care

THE ZERO YEAR

President No. 9, William Henry Harrison
Nominated at age 68
During that time he was the oldest one
That people would nominate
He happens to serve the shortest time
Only one month is all
After which, he began dying
Had to answer the roll call
1840 he was elected in
Served the shortest time you know
Until now, bad luck it's been
To win a year ending with zero
Out of all presidents listed below
Except Taylor in 1848
Died being chosen with a year ending with zero
Natural death or assassinate

William Henry Harrison 1840
Zachary Taylor 1848
Abraham Lincoln 1860
James A. Garfield 1880
William McKinley 1900
Warren G. Harding 1920
Franklin D. Roosevelt 1940
John F. Kennedy 1960

IT'S NOT THE PRESIDENT, IT'S US

We wonder why things go up so high
It's because thieves are standing by
We lay it on the president, but that's a lie
Sometimes when we hear prices, we want to cry
With no money people go into the store
First of all looking for money on the floor
If they don't find it, they'll look some more
Something from the shelf then out the door
That's why in the last thousands of days
Prices just continue to raise
When one person steals, the other one pays
While his friend's standing there giving him praise
If you want the prices to stay down
Report what you see with a low sound
The people can live better in town
The store isn't taking a loss on any ground

DOUGLAS FIR TREES

Douglas Fir is a common tree
One we should all remember
It's in the shape of a triangle
And produces lots of timber
Found in Oregon and Washington
Belonging to the Pine
Height reaches at least 200
And 250 sometimes
You may find a forest
With them spread all around
They're sometimes used for Christmas
And decorated up and down

RANGE FIRING

To become a real good expert shot
Aim the gun at the bullseye spot
Hold it tight
Line up the sight
Don't pull the trigger till you get it lined up right
When you go to the range to fire
Proper way to be the one they hire
Stand still and freeze
Trigger squeeze
Continue firing until you're truly well pleased

THOMAS WOODROW WILSON

Woodrow Wilson was president 28
Two terms he won for you and me
He was the 8th from Virginia State
And the first with a Doctors Degree
During the year of 1912
We had a Republican Split
William Howard Taft and Teddy Roosevelt
Were challenging each other for it
Roosevelt won in 1904
Taft won in 1908
Seems as though they both wanted more
But they challenged each other the wrong date
In 1912 the Republicans had two
The Democrats had Woodrow Wilson
That's the reason why with Wilson's few
Electoral votes he won

BEING FOR REAL

One thing we shouldn't do is complain
You should worship God in Jesus name
You should give the Lord your very best
And I promise you, he'll do the rest
If you can't sing, don't be a choir member
You'll be in the way from January till December
Join the prayer crew or usher band
The main thing to do being an usher is stand
Never complain about the others
Treat everyone as sisters and brothers
If someone makes an error, correct him right away
If you can't do better, you have nothing to say
When it's your turn to get up, don't mess around
When you're on program, participate and sit down
You should always keep the program moving
And you will have much better service approving

WHAT'S A LIE

A lie is anything you say false
A statement that's made untrue
After telling one, you feel like a wasp
Has put a bad sting on you
All are liars, says the bible
Because no one is good
They sometimes hurt you more than a rifle
They could do more than that, they could
Don't think because a man's a preacher
That he won't tell a lie
And others which have become new creatures
Or some things trying to get by
Many times when people try to get by
The truth, they will fail it
But you must remember, a lie is a lie
No matter who tells it

FREE AT LAST

Martin Luther King was sent from the Lord
For all that he did, he had to work hard
To get everybody on one accord
He would get down on his knees and fast

Although he knew that help was on its way
All we needed to do was get down and pray
His dream was going to come true some day
And when it did let the other stay past

On his tomb you will find these words
Which by now all should have heard
Sung together like the singing of birds
"Free at last, free at last, Thank God I'm free at last.

SOMEONE TO REMEMBER

One name to be remembered each and every day
Is Martin Luther King, Jr., I do say
He brought the blacks from a mighty long way
And proved to the whites that violence doesn't pay

The Lord is the only one he'd have to stay
With at all times while his followers would pray
He was just as comfortable as being beside a bay
His heart, in Jesus' hands, he would lay

When asked to do for his people, he never said "Nay"
Making him say no was harder than searching in hay
Early within the month before the month of May
He was shot and killed by James Earl Ray

BIRTHDAY

My birthday was August, the second
I was thirty-eight, I reckon
Looking for a dollar each year
My wife said, "You may only have a beer."

I saw with my two eyes
A very, very big surprise
For each year that she gave me two dollars
You should have heard me when I hollered

So I found out at last
Came to mind and will never pass
If you want a large amount and don't want trouble
Then keep your big mouth shut and everything will double

CHRISTMAS

I'd like to say "Good morning" to everyone here
We want you to sit down, rest back, and cheer
There's no need for anyone to fear
Just look out the window and see that the day is clear

I don't want to see not one tear
All should be happy from front to rear
Smile everyone, be happy my dear
You're going to hear something good within your ear

So go ahead and complete your root beer
Then there's something I want you to hear
I'd like to say to everyone while time is near
Merry Christmas and
A Happy New Year!!!

THE CALL IN THE FALL

One early morning as I was down on my knees
I received an early morning call
Saying we're to go to Oregon, so everyone freeze
But we're not going there to have a ball

We're going to make money by cutting down trees
And get supplies at Red Bird Mall
We will be traveling in groups of threes
Four trucks will take care of all

Everyone be sure to get your keys
We're going to make money after all
Enough to take a trip overseas
To see the Brussels City Hall

So after work, everyone was well pleased
Felt like we had knocked down the wall
And believe me some of those trees
Were three hundred and fifty (350) feet tall

As one was coming down you could see its leaves
Fell so hard that it broke the stall
Knocked a hole in the ground with the help of a breeze
The bigger they are, the harder they fall

ANNUAL CHOIR DAY

At this time I would like to say
To all who came to worship with us on Annual Choir Day
We welcome all who came from Griggs Chapel Choir
And others who came to worship here with us the next hour

We want you to listen for the next hour
To none other than Salem and Griggs Chapel Choir
Then 1 know you will be ready
For Rev. Webb to make your heart steady

If you get happy and feel you want to shout
Help yourself and ushers please don't take them out
Or if you would like to join the choir and sing
That won't do nothing but make our hearts ring

Surely, you're all welcome to give
You can do that as long as you live
If you can't do that then why not clap your hands
Then it won't be but one more thing to do, say Amen

When you are in pain and think you need help
Just come by Salem on Annual Choir Day
And listen to Rev. Webb
This day comes once a year and that's very very seldom
But believe me when it comes you are
welcome...welcome...welcome

INDEPENDENCE DAY

July 4,1981
We were visiting our boss, Mr. Wilson
We had steak, ribs, chops, all barbeque
Just at the right time for me and you

His wife was as busy as can be
In the kitchen cooking for you and me
Mr. Wilson was at the table helping his wife set it
We heard a loud voice "Come and get it"

Come on everybody, smile don't cry
Thinking Mrs. Wilson can't cook but you're a lie
She's got what it takes and that's one or some
Best cooking brains you can have 'til the day is done

Just in case there's something you need to fry
You'll get it over by turning the stove high
And we'll have something for you to eat
Remember, food ain't nothing without meat

For dessert you'll have lemon pie
And that should conclude it on the 4th of July
Last question asked "Did you get enough?"
Oh boy, Yes, and that was some good stuff

ANNUAL MEN'S DAY

We welcome you all from Greater Emmanuel
That came to worship with us on our 28th Annual
If you came to worship the Master, you're at the right place
So sit down and make yourself comfortable with a smiling
    face

I would like to say to the female only
Just because this is Men's Day don't feel lonely
You don't have to be a male to take part
Clap your hands, stomp your feet, whatever is in your heart

I would like to say to the male, too
Just in case you don't know what to do
You don't have to be a member to participate
Sing, shout, dance, whatever it takes

The main thing we want to be heard
Is none other than our Father's word
In a few moments you'll hear it come out
Of none other than the (Guest Speaker's) mouth

The last and least thing I'd like to say
Is that it's a pleasure to see you all on Men's Day
All will come back to visit with us I reckon
That's why I say you are welcome, welcome, welcome

TIGERS

Tigers are very large animals
Weighing from 4 to 600 pounds
They walk through the jungle looking for food
By trying to smell the ground

They finally come up with something
For a good meal to make
They'll catch a deer and hang with their claws
And the deer can make no escapes

Tigers come in beautiful colors
Tawny yellow with plenty of might
And over this body of theirs
They also have black stripes

A tiger is a circus animal
Who participates every year
Who do so many different tricks
By jumping far and near

In order to train a wild tiger
You must catch him when he's small
And stay with him 'til he grows up
And with him you can have a ball

THE FOUR SEASONS

I saw birds flying one day
More flew from another way
They flew in cold weather
Kept warm with their feathers
And no one was out to play

Everything is not alike
Daily you'll see different sights
How trees change is spring
Except for the evergreens
And that's when you fly a kite

In summer, you take your vacations
To see things and their locations
You travel different ways
For a certain number of days
To visit other cities in our nation

The last one to mention is fall
Fair opens and you have a ball
It hasn't been told
Fall's when it gets cold
If I need help, I'll call

YOU TOUCHED ME AND I GREW

What a wonderful time we're having here
Everyone sit down, rest back, and cheer
Everything is wonderful; nothing looks tough
I still just can't say "Thank you" enough

When somebody's helping you any time a day
Just keep your big mouth shut and let them have their way
Most of the time things will come out better than to be
A wonderful world trip all around the sea

If anyone in the world should be thankful it should be
Myself, for the Lord has made everything possible for me
Every day here I am enjoying my home
And still enjoying you over the telephone

When you need help you will find your friend
Someone who will help all the way to the end
The Lord Jesus Christ will send one or some
He sent me to Bro. and Sis. R. W. Carrington

You stay out of the way and let the Carringtons boss
Not a lot of money, but brainwork it cost
Just follow them and you will not get lost
Because they've been led by the Lord to straighten up this house

It's good to have a house you can run
Having an open house is very lots of fun
Adding it all up you will have a very large sum
You didn't lose so you automatically won

WHAT'S GOOD ABOUT BEING A CUSTODIAN

Many people don't like being custodians
They don't like cleaning behind others
Many of them don't like the salary
And all the work it covers

The custodian salary has gotten much better
Than what it used to be
They give the teachers a certain percent raise
And the custodian gets the same with thee

By going outside to clean up
Is an easy way to find money
While you're picking up the trash
You'll sometimes find something for your honey

This can also happen inside
While you're dust mopping the rooms
No telling how much you'll be done found
Before you put up your broom

CONTINUING WITH ANOTHER DAY

The very' next day on August 4
He put me on the basement floor
To wash walls starting on the north end
Going south where two doors were opened

It was more good about it, than just the air
Also at the south end, two chairs were there
I started on the north end that was very hot
And it was a long ways to the south, believe it or not

I happen to finally get to the south end
And when I did, there was a break at ten
I sat in one of the chairs all alone
Enjoying the air coming from the Lord well known

I sure did hate to have to turn around
But after going up the hall I had to come back down
I don't know what conclusions were made about the morning labour
But whatever it was, it was in my favor

WHICH IS BEST

It's always good to own your home
And pay your utility bills
Your heavy problems won't last long
When you make some good deals

When you're in an apartment, you're in trouble
Paying so much rent
You'll get the feeling that things have doubled
To see just what I meant

Renting is nothing but throwing away money
For something you'll never own
They're so high it ain't even funny
It's best to have a home

Don't tell a lie and say you can't afford to own
And you just have to rent
All you need to do to buy you a home
Is get you a down payment

You can rent for a number of years
For example, the number of ten
Then decide to buy with heep of cheers
But you must start all over again

If the city comes by for the apartment land
You'll come out empty-handed honey
If it takes your home from where it stands
You will get a piece of money

BECOMING A DIFFERENT PERSON

I once felt like a different man
Because I was making more money
Began working at South Oak Cliff School
On the parking lot, even when it was sunny

When I first got there, I would clean the lot
And then go over to the gate
To wait for students to drive in
They wouldn't hardly come before eight

Then I'd collect money from them
The amount of fifteen cents
And some didn't even want to pay that
And would park outside the fence

When school was out, I would be inside
To help custodians strip the floors
I'd stay inside the whole summer
Except vacation when they let me go

Three weeks after getting this job
The Lord blessed me with a home
Blessed me with money, furniture, and food
And also a telephone

I stayed in touch with many people
By giving them a telephone call
I stayed in touch with the LORD also
"FOR HE WAS THE ONE WHO PROVIDED ME ALL"

FREE PUNISHMENT

Once upon a time there was a total of nine men
On a yard crew
And would you believe every day they had a lot of
Work to do.

The boss man and his assistant
Were inside doing another job
They had to carry a heavy can
Filled to the top with corn on the cob

Six of the others were mowing and digging
While the other one was looking very hard
He thought he was too good
To be working out in the yard

While he was standing there looking so hard
Ants were crawling up his leg
Help! He had to beg for
And boy didn't he beg

When the boss man heard about it
One thing he did state
If you go ahead and move on
The ants you'll escape

GREETING

Once there was a young man who was very lonely
Think he didn't know anybody, but that was a bunch of bologna
He lived in an apartment on the ground floor
And his apartment number was 184

He was out in the front looking toward north
In his rocking chair, rocking back and forth
Suddenly, a ball hit him right upside the head
That came from upstairs and made him feel dead

He went upstairs to tell them what needed to be told
But when he got there, it was a young lady 20 years old
Immediately that frown changed to a big smile
And stayed that way for a nice while

When the young lady saw him she said, what's up
You hit me with your ball and I should have ducked
Oh gee, sir, I'm sorry, please have no sweat
I'm glad, otherwise, we wouldn't have met

THE LEVINE COUPLE

Many things we know were taught by Indians
The leader of that bunch was Mrs. Lillian
You have a head and knows how to use it
That which you don't know, ask Louis

Bro. Levine will help you all he can with pleasure
It makes him feel like he was great treasure
His work really shows you how he has felt
But if you offer to help him, he'll have a fit and melt

I promise you in this picture there's no fraction
These two really, really put their love into action
You can always see that they are your friends
And will remain if you let them sleep at ten

Bro. Louis Levine treats me as a brother
Sis. Lillian Levine treats me as a mother
One thing that's very hard to say
Is the surprise they have in store for you any day

THE GREATEST THREE

Out of all Presidents of the United States
There are three we would put before any other one
One is a Republican and two are Democrats
Franklin Roosevelt, Abraham Lincoln, and Thomas Jefferson

Franklin Roosevelt led us through World War 2
No need for us to try and conceal
He created jobs to give the people something to do
That worked perfectly along with his New Deal

Some call Lincoln the best, some call him a brother
Without an education, he ended up brave
Led us through the only war we had with each other
And had nerve to free the slaves

Thomas Jefferson, in 1796, was defeated
And came back very strong
Democratic-Republican was the party he treated
And stayed there eight years long

These are supposed to be the greatest three
Presidents we've ever had in history
Someday we might find someone to match thee
But they'll have to give a sharp victory

You'll find these men on money pieces
The face of Lincoln you'll find on two
That's because historians call him the greatest
With such little he knew

REV. HERMAN WARNER

I'd like to tell you about a Christian man
Who never tries to hide
I will admit, he's a Cowboy fan
But when it's time for church, that's aside

You don't get to hear him much
But he really knows the word
You can get the real touch
From what you'll be done heard

His preaching will give you a lift
Of that you'll need
And make you want to use your gift
In church, yes indeed

A man who really serves the Master
And never hides in a corner
Is Salem Baptist Church Assistant Pastor
Rev. Herman Warner

WELCOME TO THE CONWAY HOUSE

We appear here today with happiness in our hearts
To see what you have and how much farther you have to
    go
You've made one of the highest steps that people make on
    earth
But this is not half of what you must do you know

By looking at the house and trees, and to see how much
    you're pleased
Give proof to each of us that you've been on your knees
And shall Bro. Conway enjoy his new home
And still enjoy you all over the telephone

APPRECIATION FOR SIS. L. F. CHEATOM

I appear here today without a greenback dollar
I have not one bill down from foot up to collar
But I didn't come here broke to this religious palace
I did come happy as every life in Dallas

You'll be happy when it rains there will be no dear pains
The truth will make you free when it stays in your brains
And shall Rev. L. F. Cheatom of True Gospel yet Pastor
Not one cent for you but many millions for the Master

You don't see it so much not everyone has nerve
To stand before an audience to worship the Lord and serve
Some try to dodge the Lord by staying in home
For that you'll be punished 'cause His word must go on

Not only you but the bird listening to my God's Word
It can't help you at all unless it's really heard
So shall Rev. L. F. Cheatom of True Gospel yet preach
Not only here but as far as can reach

BEST IS YET TO COME

Five teenage boys worked at a school
Four stayed together to tease
The other one they tried to play a fool
But he was always well pleased

Once he was sent into the heat
To go around and pick up trash
The same day he took a treat
From the others by being harassed

One day they all made a laugh
He didn't think it was so funny
While cleaning the yard, he found some cash
A good size piece of money

As the boss was choosing another man
He quickly said "No, let me"
You sure you don't want to stay in with the fan
Just as sure as I can be

MOTHER'S DAY

I reminded Mrs. Terrel of our church
Who way ninety six (96) years old
That we were going to put something in her purse
And it won't be silver or gold

I'm sure it will be a help to you
To take off some financial weight
Oh no! there is too much to do
So we may add a cake

And it will be your big gift
On the thirteenth (13) of May
We hope it will give you a lift
To make it through this Mother's Day

IS THERE ANYONE ANY BETTER

There was a young lady in Texas; school board knew they
    would need her
As they all got together and took her out to feed her
I know one thing, this young lady was an excellent reader
And still is, I know to say' some people call her Ouida

She was elected Director of Legislation and still is today
And happens to be past President of the P.T.A.
There's no one who can match her, so that she'll stay
So now we'll all sit back and listen to Fae

She's just the same at her church, Sunday School T
And sings in one of the choirs just like me
To make yourself comfortable, go drink a cup of coffee
And have for your company none other than Mrs. Lee

Last and least you just don't know how happy you'll be
And feel like getting on a ship, sailing across the sea
To meet the most kindest woman living in the Big D
And that could be none other than the Great Mrs. Ouida
    Fae Lee

THE NEW WEDDED COUPLE

One spring morning on a sunny day
My darling and I camped by the bay
She asked me if I felt good in a way
I said "So far, so good, so well understood"

We were happy to see each other
I really and truly loved her as a mother
She was as close to me as a brother
We knew everything was going straight and good

Now that we had settled down
True love I knew I had found
She asked "What's going on" with a loveable sound
I said "Nothing much, nothing good, nothing goes the way
      it should

In love we both quickly fell
Many people we did tell
We could just hear the wedding bells
Ringing as loud as they could

CAROL GOODWIN

I know a young lady that works at SOC
In the main office, believe it or not
Her name is none other than Carol Goodwyn
Her favorite food is banana pudding

She drives a Bonneville, every day
That she bought, for herself, last May
You can tell when she is near
The best-looking employee at SOC this year

Every day she's on the main floor
And doesn't leave till half past four
I don't see why she won't go to the palace
And volunteer to run for Miss Dallas

There's no way how she would lose
She has knowledge everyone could use
No one's offering a job, no use
Because SOC isn't going to turn her loose

THE HOLY BIBLE

I know of a weapon stronger, than rifle
This weapon is none other than the Bible

You can use this weapon any time, anywhere
It's one that won't fail you; everyone should care

There should be a Bible in everybody's home
Can still be used as a weapon when everyone's gone

The smallest library in the world but the very best
It can fill you up with honest righteousness

The Bible is very true to one hundred per cent
No way you can change it, read to a certain extent

This is one thing that there will always be
Jesus is the Son who will always be with thee

THE CREATION

In the beginning was the creation
God put everything in its location
He made first the Heavens and Earth
No one knows how much it's really worth

To have light, he made the sun
It's amazing, he didn't need but one
To shine on the whole earth
And was doing it before the first birth

He made the beautiful flowers and trees
And also the large rivers and seas
He put in the water some wild beast
And he hadn't yet ceased

You can look out each night and see the stars
That you see from other Planets, including Mars
Along with the stars, sets the moon
You can sometimes see it at noon

On the sixth day he made man
To come and watch over his land
We all should give the Lord praise
For making everything in six days

WHAT BUILDS UP A CHURCH

First you should give everyone something to do
But let it be a choice of their own
If they want to do nothing, then let them warm the pew
And hear everything needs to be known

Don't have choir members that can't read music
Don't have teachers that can't read
When it's time for a leader, let the members choose it
They know who they want and who they need

Don't have deacons that haven't been ordained
They will only be in the way
Don't have leaders that haven't been trained
They'll mess you up any day

Try to use one hundred percent your young ones
Don't wait till holidays to do so
Teach them how to pray, teach and lead songs
And that will make them want to do more

LEARN TO THANK THE LORD

The Lord has done so much for us
All have something to be thankful for
I know it says "Ask and it shall be given"
"Knock and ye shall open the door"

If you have a total of ninety-nine cents
Don't ask the Lord to make it a dollar
Thank Him for the ninety-nine cents
And He'll bless you before tomorrow

If you're forty-nine years of age
And your birthday's the first of May
Don't ask the Lord to let you see it
Thank Him for this day

Everyone should get on his knees and pray
Things we should pray for are very many
What we have to ask Him for is nothing
What we have to thank Him for is plenty

IT PAYS TO KNOW GOD

It's always good to have a friend
Someone to help you around
But no one will stay to the end
But will sometimes turn you down

Sad hearts will come to others
To you it may take longer
Continue to honour your sisters and brothers
Prove that you are stronger

The Lord's way is always right
Following it you'll be correct
Nothing beats being in Christian light
But you ain't heard nothing yet

Pray for the ones which mistreat you
You will receive your reward
You pray for the wrong things you do
But it pays to know the Lord

THE BIRTH OF CHRIST

Let me tell you something about our Master
That I'm sure you've heard from your Pastor
Late one night lying in a manger
Filled with hay and around no anger

There was Jesus with his Mother, Mary
Joseph was there and no one was weary
Shepherds were around watching their flock
Cattle woke Jesus, the same as the clock

And there shining in the East
Was the brightest star that would never cease
Three wise men from very far
Found Jesus by the light of the star

Came to worship Him on camel backs
And brought gifts to Jesus in sacks
The gifts were myrrh, frankincense, and gold
There's much to be told

THE HOLY LAND

Every year people have ideas planned
To go and visit the Holy Land
So they can walk where their Master walked
And also talk where their Master talked

Where they can pray with righteousness
And see the tomb where He rests
And see the place He did rise
And the Jordan River, where he was baptized

Seeing this won't make you a better Christian
You'll have to continue your mission
Giving you a better thought it could
Of being a Christian the way you should

But that's really left up to you
Of whether or not you want to
I'm sure the people enjoy the tour and weather
I'm sure they'll enjoy heaven much better

PRECIOUS AIR FROM THE LORD

After a good birthday on August the Second
Happiness was all over, I reckon
When I got to work on August third
Trouble had already been stirred

The boss man told me to put out the water hose
After I got started, his assistant arose
Telling me that there was a flood upstairs
That's what I get for cheering for the South Oak Cliff Bears

When I got up there it was very hot
I knew that I was at a bad spot
You couldn't see nothing on me but sweat
Dripping from everywhere, including my neck

After that I had to remove one hose
And put it on a patio where pretty grass grows
While we were out there trying to connect the stuff
A good wind was coming and that was enough

The assistant kept having to go back and forth
Getting supplies while the wind was coming from the north
He never did come up with the right tool
But using up the time helped me get cool

Some of that sweat did disappear
And boy I was happy, filled up with cheer
I couldn't say nothing but "Thank you" to Him
I felt cool enough to swing from a limb

PRAYER BEFORE CRUCIFIXION

Jesus went out into the Garden of Gethsemane
Along with His disciples, all twelve
To say a word of prayer unto His Father
And on His face He fell

He took along with Him Peter
And the two sons of Zebedee
And He went a little farther to pray
Asking His Father to let His cup pass from me

In Just the short time He was gone
He came back and found them asleep
The spirit is indeed willing
But the flesh is weak

After He had prayed the second time
He already knew their fate
And upon His return
He found none of them awake

He went away for the third time
Finding them asleep again was hard to believe
One thing they just didn't recognize
Was that this night was Crucifixion Eve

TIME TO PRAY

As you go to bed each night, you should pray
Thanking the Lord for blessing you all the way
You shouldn't ask him to let you live to see tomorrow
Without thanking Him for carrying you through your sorrows

All prayers are answered, but may not be the way you see
God overlooketh no one when they are in need of thee
He still has His very first time to be late
He's always on time and He's always straight

To everyone, you should get on your knees and bow
We all need the Lord and we need Him right now
He's the only one who will never turn you down
He will send you blessings from all around

We all have blessings at very high amounts
Total so high, you can't even count
He is still blessing everyone today
That's why we should all get on our knees and pray

WORSHIPPING THE LORD

Everyone should want to serve the Lord
And all should be of one accord
Church is the place where everyone could take part
And have everything coming from the heart

Have different troops to lead prayer
Every Sunday, pick a new pair
It will be so no one will be ashamed
To say a word of prayer in Jesus' name

Always begin your service on time
Don't wait for anyone that's out of line
And if so many interruptions be docked
So many people wouldn't have to watch the clock

On the first Sunday, have the Lord's Supper
Like they did in the upper
Remember it represents the body and blood
And always will be a remembered flood

A CHRISTIAN FAMILY

I once met a man walking down the alley
Had a nice home in Mill Valley
Said he was a Christian and feels merry
He is known as Alfred Huntsberry

His wife's name is Huntsberry, Alma
They have two daughters, Kashenia and Cassandra
And a son, they call him Wendell
They all love each other, you can easily tell

Another name for them would be "Receivers Blessing"
You can tell when someone's a child of the King
By the way he treats others
Pray, shout and sing

Once you're with the Lord, you're going to stay
And work for Him anytime, any day
Someday they'll receive their gift above
From their own Father who puts in action His love

LOCATION MEANS A LOT

The Lord knows all your needs
And all your wants, too
He's the one to help you succeed
And do what you want to do

I'm handicapped and can't drive
It would be too dangerous for me
If I want to stay alive
I better let the car go free

I bought a home in '79
Right next door to a church
With plenty more down the line
And walking distance of work

I'm one block away from a grocery store
When I'm hungry and need to eat
Instead of driving a car to go
I can always use my feet

A cleaners is one block of me
I'm one block of a school
Another bus stop is behind me, gee
So I won't have to ride a mule

V.A. Hospital is three blocks away
One and a half from washaterias
It isn't too much more to say
And I don't have to make it so serious

Since I truly can't drive
My help cometh from the Lord
He fixed it where I could survive
If I stay on his Word

SERVING THE LORD

When you go to church to serve
The Lord will give you what you deserve
Don't I assure you, you do your best
And I assure you He'll do the rest

Don't ever let the people bother you
No matter who's there, the Lord's there too
Makes no difference how many's on the list
One thing I do know, God is in the midst

You should sing out with what few
People you have, if it's one or two
Tell your people to sing out loud
Because it doesn't take a crowd

When you've got Jesus, you've got it all
He's the one to answer your call
I've been a witness since we've met
Because He hasn't failed me yet

When you do someone a favor, don't look for one
Your blessings from the Lord will come
Whatever you did for the other human being
The blessing from the Lord will be a bigger thing

THE HAPPIEST TIME OF MY LIFE

Something good must be going and I can't speak it
I want you all to know how much I appreciate it
I love you all and God above
It makes me feel good to see you all here with love

You know how I feel with all of you here
I can also tell you that God is near
I hope you all come see me again
Don't wait till the Lord takes me in

I see how easy the spirit goes
I look at each of you and knows
How happy you are for being here
With love, joy, peace and cheers

Though this open house has been a strife
The happiest time of my life
And don't you forget we had a house warming
We had it at night and not in the morning

ALL THINGS ARE POSSIBLE

There's nothing impossible for you to do
If you really want to participate
With God, all things are possible for you
He can make no mistakes

He will bring you safely through
As He opens the doors of the gates
If there's something you need with filthy loot
A hand from Him it takes

If you want a car or a canoe
And on minimum wages this date
Just put a little hustling in what you do
Because it's not the amount of money you make

You must know that this is true
There's not much time to wait
And not much help, only a few
They do better than others this date
 If you do the right thing, too
 You'll be better off than your mate

IDENTICAL CHAPTERS

II Kings 19 and Isaiah 37
Read the same word almost
It tells you about a man name Hezekiah
What he was doing at his post.

16 verses in both of the chapters
Read exactly the same way
The rest has one or two words different
Where in Kings you see one, Isaiah a

It would be a pleasure looking at them
Finding the different words would be fun
And you will feel you have worked a puzzle
When you have found everyone

THE FIERY FURNACE

Nebuchadnezzar intended to be obeyed
And everyone to worship him down on their knees
And for them to all fall down, kneel and freeze
Wanted to be king and for it to be okayed
Three Hebrew boys ignored him and they truly paid
A big price by the king for ignoring fees
It was being thrown in a furnace without breeze
After being thrown in the fiery furnace, they prayed

The fiery furnace truly was extremely hot
You may think it was three in there, but it was not
It happened to be four and the fourth was the Lord
That's why they were unharmed; they were on one accord
If you know to let the Lord be in control
You know everything that needs to be told

THANK GOD FOR EVERYTHING

O give thanks unto my God
Which comfort me with thy rod
Who gives me a place to live
And blesses me so I can give

He keeps me walking on my feet
And gives me food so I can eat
He lets me drink water, also
Give me hands to touch, you know

He gives me eyes that I may see
And ears to hear, he gives to me
And he gives me a nose to smell
And a choice of heaven or hell

We thank you for your son with love
Who died for all that is born of
Water and spirit when born again
Cause Jesus died for all our sins

BIRTH OF CHRIST

Jesus was born in Bethlehem
It happened to be a cold night
It happened to also be dark
But the stars were just so bright

Shepherds were in the field close by
An angel brought them the good news
Saying "Go and see the newborn Saviour"
They went, and did not refuse

They left the field and went to town
And they went all together
To see baby Jesus with his mother
In a barn in some real cold weather

And they happened to find the THING
Lying in a manger on hay
And they left full of joy and praises
Cause for them it was a happy day

HOW LONG WAS JONAH IN THE WHALE

God gave Jonah an order to go
To Ninevah but he went to Tarshish
And his disobedience made him
Quickly be swallowed up by a fish

He was punished for disobedience
God truly kept him out of sight
He was in the belly of the whale
For three long days and three nights

He was in there for what we call
A full day and a half a day
He was happy to be spat out
After he happened to pray

Jesus was in the grave also
Same time like the gospels say (Matthew 12:40)
You realize back in those days
Any part of a day was a day

CHRISTMAS DINNER

It is now time for the blessing
Then let's have some turkey and dressing
If not, then you can have some ham
Along with some good candied yams

It won't be completed without greens
Then let's have one or two more things
Such as having some pumpkin pie
You just won't believe your eye

You'll have so much food and punch
You can set some aside for tomorrow's lunch
By time you get completely through
You'll feel just like somebody new

MARCH ON WASHINGTON

On August 28, 1963
The capitol, Washington, D.C.
Looking for some peace and liberty
And love among humans like you and me

Martin Luther King was very proud
On Lincoln Memorial speaking loud
Facing a real nice huge crowd
Just before he started, he bowed

Quarter of a million heard Dr. King
Say his biggest speech, I Have A Dream
He knew integration, it would bring
One of the most important things

He mentioned "Some day this country will rise"
If we only be very wise
To see happy tears and cries
You will not believe your eyes

DEATH OF MARTIN LUTHER KING, JR.

Before the death of Martin Luther King
He was in Memphis, Tennessee preparing
A march for sanitation workers driving
To a better amount of wealth

He knew he was going to be killed
But he continued to do God's will
Continued to speak for the right until
He had taken his last breath

April 4 was a very bad day
Everyone happened to cry out "Nay"
When they heard all about James Earl Ray
Putting Martin Luther King to death

LEAP YEAR

Every four years there is a leap year
So when one leaves, another one's near
February 29, fog or clear
Is when we get the extra day

23 hours and 56 minutes
Spins the world and everything in it
Brings one full day as the Lord spins it
And we continue to pray

One day equals 24 hours
That happens to be man time power
Four minutes over for extra showers
Brings leap year all the way

THE BUS BOYCOTT

December 1, 1955
There happened to be no jive
When Martin Luther King made his first move
To try and keep everything smooth

Rosa Parks sat at the front of the bus
The white folks tried to make a big fuss
By throwing her in the city jail
All alone in one hot cell

While she was in there getting hot
Dr. King put on a bus boycott
That made the city of Montgomery go broke
And to the whites this was no joke

And kept it going all through the town
Until they took these bus signs down
And believe me, not that they had to
Broke as they got, they were more than glad to

All other cities had the bus signs moved
And decided to keep things very smooth
They could easily see that wrong doesn't win
So they never put up those bus signs again

THE LONGEST MARCH IN THE WORLD

Martin Luther King, Jr. and his troop
Made a pretty good huge size group
Though it wasn't too good of a sight
To see them walking day and night

Selma, Alabama was the beginning
Montgomery, Alabama was the ending
50,000 was the amount of folks
Walking this distance to register to vote

The sight truly did not look good
But they did do the best they could
Dogs were sicked on them while they walked
Water on them but they didn't halt

But when they did finally get there
Martin Luther King spoke in the air
Letting them know we're citizens, too
And voting is something we want to do

Martin Luther King spoke a real good speech
A very high goal he was trying to reach
And he did hit the high goal at last
Him, and his very huge size cast

ASSASSINATION OF JFK

On the 22nd day of November
In the year of 1963
Is something we will always remember
That happened right here in Big D

Kennedy was in a Lincoln car
Passing by, waving at the crowd
Although he didn't get very far
Before a noise was heard out loud

Three shots as a trigger was pulled
Nearly put him to his death
One of them went straight through his skull
And he lost all of his breath

They rush him out on Harry Hines
To a hospital named Parkland
But they couldn't get him there in time
And the whole nation was darkened.

This poem was written on November 22, 1996

BLACK BARBECUE HOUSES

This is Black History Month
Know what we all should do
Take a day off this month
And get some barbecue

They have sliced beef, links,
Long and short ribs, too
This is only half of
What they have for you

Not too many dollars it takes
It only take a few
To fill your body up
Feels good when you get through

There is always someone best
Would you like to know who
You'll never find no one better
Then Hardeman's Barbecue

THE LITTLE MOST LOVABLE LACY

Little Mrs. Lacy happens to be
The best looking teacher of the city
A very well talented person is she
And everyone knows she's so pretty

A pretty lady that works at SOC
And dresses so nice, also
Like Mrs. Tolbert, believe it or not
You'll find them both on the first floor

She happens to be a Homemaking Teacher
Teaching school children how to sew
And lots of other things you do as house features
All of it you'll need to know

Sometime she's in the next door room
Teaching lots of children how to cook
Things like meat, vegetables, and prunes
Without always using a cookbook

ALWAYS ON TIME

Once there was a fire that was so bad
The scenes of everything sure looked sad
The family was losing all that they had
They went on the outside of the gate

The fire department quickly got a call
Then they jumped on the wagon after all
While the house just continued to fall
From a family of a total of eight (8)

After they went outside to the rear
The fire happened to be drawing near
Hoping that the firemen would get here
Because they could no longer wait

The fire fighters were blocked by a train
But the Lord sent a big heavy rain
The fire disappeared with no serious pains
The Lord was on time cause he's never late

DAYLIGHT SAVINGS TIME

How many days are there in a year
There are three hundred and sixty-five
Do all have twenty-four hours here
Or does it change while you 're alive

Twenty-four hours we give to all days
Which go FROM 12:01 to 12
Each one of them we give the Lord praise
For keeping us out of hell

All days a year have twenty-four hours
Except two which you subtract
And this is done by all man power
One you set up and the other back.

WHAT STOPS TRAFFIC

A person can be up on his feet
Walking a good mile down the street
All kinds of people he will meet
In sunshine or drizzles of rain

But he must let the traffic go by
Or maybe he will surely die
Or could be hurt while he lies
On the ground or in serious pain

Could a funeral stop traffic, yes
Coming down any street, I guess
The funeral keeps on going, unless
They hear a siren in the lane

The funeral will stop for the siren
Because they know what that means
Robbery, fire, or death in scene
So far, everything is plain

Red lights, you see the police drive through
For protection of me and you
Sometimes you may see a large crew
But they must stop for the train.

MILITARY OFFICERS

Lieutenants start the officers out low
That's why they have to go very far
They have to go a real good distance
In order to remove that bar

Captains have their bars doubled
And they wear two silver ones
They keep the sergeants out of trouble
By telling them what needs to be done

A major, we will make it brief
His identity is a golden leaf
Lieutenant Colonel wears a silver one
Up until the job is done

A colonel's rank is very high
A silver eagle by and by
He has to be a real good guy
To rank like this before he die

Generals, from one to five stars
Drive in mighty fantastic cars
Fighting for us in foreign wars
Here in the United States

THE GREAT SOPRANO VOICE LADY

One lady which Salem Baptist Church really admire
Is one who's used to singing in the Senior Choir
This is one lady who can really sing out your brain
You should know her by now, her name is Hewitt, Loraine

This woman does have a good soprano voice
And one who is able to make you rejoice
I will admit that this woman is very loud
She can't hide her voice, matters the size of crowd

If you're in the choir and you're not very good
Stand next to her for help and stay like you should
Listen very carefully to every word she says
Next time the chorus goes around, join in with praise

You really should not try to be as loud as she
If any mistakes are made, you it cannot be
Rehearsal or in service while singing the song
Long as they can't hear you, you cannot be wrong

LYNDON BAINES JOHNSON

Lyndon Johnson took over late in 63
After the death of President Kennedy
In Texas, the state which he was born in
Happened to be the one which he was sworn in

He was another working with civil rights
Because he was trying to help black and white
The voting rights of southern blacks made protection
After he okayed it and made connection

He would listen to others when it was for the best
Throughout his full term, helped Dr. King make success
By okaying good laws which had to do with race
That hadn't already been passed to a certain base

One thing that really made this man so great
He treated all people humanity and straight
Although, he was criticized just like others
But to him we were all sisters and brothers

COMPARE LINCOLN AND WASHINGTON

Everyplace you find President Lincoln
You'll find George Washington, also
Both of them you will find on money
On a penny and a quarter, you know

Up in the State of South Dakota
You'll find them upon Mount Rushmore
Along with Jefferson and Roosevelt
Which will give you a total of four

In many cities you have named after them
Totals of elementary and high schools
Where you find the children trying to learn
Obey and live according to the rules

There's the Washington Monument in D.C.
The Lincoln Memorial's 1/4 of a mile away
Both of these men were born in February
But Lincoln died on my brother's birthday

HOW DID SOUTH OAK CLIFF BECOME NO. 1

Twice in a row SOC received the gift
To help them out on their Christmas shift
In that case everything is not so stiff
When you have someone to make it plain

South Oak Cliff called upon Mr. Tubbs
Who use to play for Chicago Cubs
After which he would put up light bulbs
On the post in the middle of the lane

Teachers are very glad to keep this man
Helps put extra money in their hand
They know we can do it like others can
But truly not until Mr. Tubbs came

We all hope to see this man next year
If so, we want the teachers to cheer
One things we will know if he's here
SOC will be No.1 school again

                To A Special Man
                Pride of SOC

WHAT TRAVELS THE FARTHEST

What in the world travels the farthest
Could it happen to be an airplane
Could go to another continent
And in three hours then hit the lane.

Or could it happen to be light
The main thing which travels so fast
Which you use always day and night
In every day which comes to pass

It takes you anywhere you know
Wherever you would like to go
It's sometime high, it's sometimes low
And always traveling to and fro

It travels anywhere at home
It travels from Dallas to Rome
A Southwestern Bell Telephone
Is the right answer to be

REDWOODS

Redwood trees are found out west
When it comes to heights they are the best
Because they 're taller than all the rest
And give lots of timber, too

They really give a most distinct height
From a far distance and a beautiful sight
Especially when the day is bright
And the sky is clear and blue

It has lots of width on the land
You can really see it as it stands
You can be in Northern California and
Look at the cars drive through

HOW DOES A TIGER FIND ITS FOOD

Tigers get so hungry in the jungle
Which you also call the wild
But they are very smart animals
They could make everything look brand

Sometimes they walk through the jungle
As they walk and smell the ground
They take their time and moved quite slowly
In a short time food they've found

Or they '11 stay close to the water
Waiting on a good size deer
And when it comes for a good drink
The tiger'll eat him without fear

LAKE ERIE

Lake Erie is the fourth of the Great Lakes
When it all comes to size
But it is surrounded by four states
Forty to sixty miles wide

It just so happens to only be
Two hundred and ten feet deep
So it is truly a shallow sea
For North America to keep

It has real strong waves for this reason
And is always stirred by storms
Which continue on through every season
Through all of the happy charms

New York and Pennsylvania's on the lake
Michigan and Ohio,
But what makes everything so great
Canada touches it, also

MORE LAND THAN WATER

Water covers over seventy percent
Of the land you see on earth
Thirty percent is seven continents
You don't know how much they're worth

Nine times out often you would believe
That there is not much land
Where trees grow and life is received
By humans as they stand

Of course, there will always be more
Land instead of water
Water covers much land you know
We only live on one quarter

BLUE RIDGE MOUNTAINS

From the northern part of Georgia
To the southern Pennsylvania
You would want to go look at
A scene and I don't blame you

There are beautiful sceneries
Ready and waiting for you
There are many miles of mountains
They're all the color of blue

You'll do yourself a big favor
By staying on this line
Somewhere in North Carolina
The highest peak you'll find

These are truly not the highest
But they're so beautiful
They were made by the good Lord
Who's always mighty dutiful

This is one of the main scenes
That you will find back east
Blue Ridge Mountains o'er Virginia
And six other states at least

WHAT A BLESSING

A blessing is a gift received from God
Who comforts you with his staff and rod
Whether you know it or not I will say
That we are truly blest each and every day

There's not a day that passes by we're not blest
Not only just today but all of the rest
He blesses us to see days we've never seen before
And certainly we will never see any more

God doesn't just jump up and give a blessing to you
First you must do what the Lord want you to do
You'll receive blessings, but first you must obey
And do anything in the world the Lord says

I'd like to say this as a human fact
Whatever he gives you he never takes back
Before you ever ask him he already knows
And when you're blest by the Lord, it really shows

FRUIT OF THE SPIRIT

Our main goal is to make it in
Heaven after being free from sin
To enter you must surely inherit
All nine of the Fruit of Spirit

To everyone you must have love
Like Jesus showed you with his blood
If you do then you will have peace
All of your life 'til you're deceased

Have faith so that you can always believe
To have blessings from the Lord to receive
And that's the thing that will give you joy
And you won't have any one to annoy

And to everyone, be meek
Always remember to everyone speak
Be gentle to everyone, act right
The Lord will bless you day and night

You're close to God when you suffer long
He's the one who makes us strong
And he's the one that's always good
Us too, if we do like we should

Be temperate and slow to anger
And it will keep you out of danger
The Fruit of Spirit must be obeyed
Cause your reward in heaven has been paid

THE JORDAN RIVER

The Jordan River is pretty good in size
Happens to be where our Master was baptized
The river flows through the Sea of Galilee
And it also empties into the Dead Sea

Children of Israel by Joshua were led
Over the river emptying into the Dead
And Joshua led them to the Promised Land
As they all entered it together hand by hand

The Jordan River has lots of history
Which always will be remembered by you and me
Reading about it tells you all the story
But believing it fills you up with glory

THE BURING BUSH

The Lord appeared unto Moses
In a bush that filled with flames
In a short period of time
He called Moses out by name

Although Moses heard the call
And answered him "Here am I"
Although he wasn't too far
Away from Mount Sinai

Even though the fire continued
The flames of course resumed
But when it had gone out
The bush was not consumed

And Moses then wondered why
The bush did never burn
It was because an angel
Of the Lord in a flame returned

THE TEN LEPERS

Once through Samaria and Galilee
Ten men were there that had leprosy
They all went to Jesus to be healed
As they all fell on their knees and kneeled

While they were all down they said to him
For the Master to have mercy on them
Next thing you know they were all made whole
Felt like they had received a new soul

As they all left one happened to come back
And said, "Thanks to you Lord for doing that"
Jesus asked him where are the other nine
I can't speak for anyone's soul but mine

THE RIVER

One of the most important rivers
Is located in Asia, southwest
Happens to be the Euphrates
And one of the longest, I guess

It happens to rise in a mountainous
Area of Turkey where the wind's strong
It does not have too much depth
And it's 1700 miles long

Large ships can't sail up and down the river
'Cause of its shallow waters and sand bars
This river has lots of history
Some peaceful and some of its' wars

The world's first civilization
Was developed around the Euphrates
The King made a decree beyond it
Of what we call the greatest

RED SEA CROSSING

The Israelites were trying to get away
From the Egyptians that were at the Red Sea
They were doing their best to try to be free
They didn't know anything to do nor say
The Children of Israel thought that their last day
Had come upon them from what they could see
Even though this is one thing that shouldn't be
Because the children always knew they could pray

God informed Moses to stretch out his hand
To divide the sea and make it dry land
Moses did and the children went across
The sea after God let them know who's boss
Then the waters came fiercely pouring down
And all the Egyptian Army was drowned

GETHSEMANE

At the foot of Mount of Olives
Is a place named Gethsemane
Happens to be a place of interest
If not, then there isn't any

There was an orchard attached to it
Figs and olives used for shade
This is the garden where our Master
Took his disciples and prayed

He happens to take along with him
Peter and sons of Zebedee
As he went farther to pray alone
Asking to move this cup from me

It was filled up with olive trees
Back during the time of Christ
But this is where our Master prayed
Before he paid the price

WHO IS THY NEIGHBOR

There in Jerusalem fell a man among thieves
They wounded him badly and decided to leave
First they stripped him all the way from toe to head
Next thing you know they made him feel dead

Then upon him there was coming a priest
He saw him and passed on by him at least
After the priest, a Levite happened to pass
Looked upon him and left away fast

Next a Samaritan happened to come
Sent from the Lord to get the job done
Took care of the wounds on the man's skin
After that he brought him to an inn

Then he gave some money to the host
Said "Do what you can for him at the most
If that's not enough, I'll bring you other"
See how a friend sticketh closer than a brother

BLIND MAN HEALED

Once there was a man who was born blind
He didn't have sight so he couldn't find
He could think because he had his mind
He hadn't done a sin of any kind

Jesus knew he was to do God's will
In that case the man had to be healed
Jesus did not keep anything concealed
From disciples who knew his works were real

I must do the Lord's work while it's day
No man can work at night, I do say
At this time I will do as I may
So he spit on the ground and made clay

In the Siloam Pool, clean thy face
Then you can see from place to place
One thing you should know in any case
Know that you've been healed by God's Grace

JOB

The Bible speaks of a perfect man
Who happens to own a lot of land
And he did own lots of cattle, too
That's why he had lots of work to do

Job happens to be the good man's name
The Land of Uz is from where he came
He eschewed evil and feared God
Being comforted with his staff and rod

God put Job up to his very best
Decided to give him a test
But Job decided not to curse
Because it would only make things worse

And he lost everything that he had
And that truly made him feel so bad
But Job decided to hear the Lord's voice
Obeyed by making the correct choice

And then by the Lord, Job was truly blessed
And was filled all over with righteousness
He doubled everything he had before
And Job ended up having twice more

FAITH

One thing that will do for us all
Faith from the Lord I do recall
He will not suffer you to fall
Just like the Bible said

Prayer and faith go together
Sometimes feel light as feathers
You should keep both forever
Pray before going to bed

To have faith you must believe
Not always ready to receive
He'll bless you before you leave
With him you'll be rightfully led

But faith you must always keep
Never put your works to sleep
Remember that we are his sheep
Faith without works is dead

THE CRUCIFIXION

Late one Friday evening in the Holy Land
On Mount Calvary, Jesus bore his cross
That's exactly where they drove nails in his hands
And everything was dark but not lost

They hung him up real high in between two thieves
For them too he was paying the price
He quickly said to one who believed
Today be with me in Paradise

They also drove nails deep in his feet
And upon his head they placed a crown
You could easily see where they had beat
Him all over and the blood came down

Right there before his own dear mother
Jesus suffered for all of us and died
Man's insurance would never cover
Death of our Savior being crucified

ROME

The capital and chief city
Of Italy happens to be Rome
At the time of Christ's ministry
Tiberius was on a throne

First it was a kingdom,
An empire now a city
It has many scenes for you
A place they keep so pretty

It was found on the Tiber River
Long centuries before Christ
You wouldn't believe the city now
Because it looks so nice

Two of Paul's letters were written
After he was free and left Rome
All were written after conversion
And now he's gone home

However in 64 A.D.
Much of Rome was destroyed
By fire that was set
By Nero who worked hard

These might have been rumors
So Nero could rebuild
A new colossal palace
And probably built of steel

THE LORD'S DAY

Sunday is The Lord's Day
A time when we should pray
If you worship him only
You will never feel lonely
And with him you will stay

Even though he made them all
On him you can always call
Go to church on Sunday
The day before Monday
Serve him everywhere you fall

Don't wait till Sunday to do
Everyday he blesses you
Believe in his word
As it's being heard
Serve him at home, too

Everything about him's good
Go to church like you should
And always take part
Directly in your heart
With him you'll be understood

HOW LONG HAS JESUS BEEN

Long as there's been a God
There's been a Jesus, too
Long centuries before
He saved both me and you

It's just that God wanted
To send him here in flesh
To help the human man
Get filled with righteousness

Pharisees did their best
To find in him some fault
But Jesus continually did
Exactly what he ought

Why was Jesus able
To open eyes of blind
Take care of all sickness
Healing all sorts of kind

He was in B.C. time
Working before being born
That way he told the people
My father and I are one

THE PROPHET DANIEL

There was a prophet Daniel
Who was real close to the Lord
There also was King Darius
Who tried to make it hard

For refusing to serve man
He was cast in the lions den
But never was he afraid
From the moment he entered in

He did let the people know
That he would not be harmed
And he didn't even feel
Not even a bit alarmed

He spent the whole night there
After people gave him warning
But there wasn't even a scratch
From that time until morning

The king came early next morning
And saw that Daniel was free
Daniel said "The Lord had come
And shut the lions mouth from me"

Daniel said "King live forever
Nothing held against these men"
They took those who accused Daniel
Said "Let's see how you like it in"

TALKING TO GOD

We know Lord there's nothing could be
Closer to sinners which includes me
Friend to everyone on land and sea
That's why we should all stay with Thee

You are closer to us than our shade
With your hands on us you have laid
Your word's sharper than any type blade
You do the healing; doctor gets paid

You sent your only begotten Son
Who came to die for everyone
On the day we didn't see the sun
We also knew victory was won

We should be living happy days
Cause living with you truly pays
Happiness we continue to raise
If we only give you the praise

WHERE SHOULD WE BE ON SUNDAY

All Christians should be in church on Sunday
We owe it to the Lord
We will truly be at work on Monday
On the job to work hard

But we should not just only be there
But there are things we must do
Worship and give to the one who cares
A lot for me and you

Sunday is the day our Master rose
From the grave to his feet
If we give, go to church, and the church grows
Our work will be complete

JUST BELIEVE

Once upon a time at the Tiberias Sea
Seven men went fishing together
Out in the water as you can see
In some nice warm spring weather

Even though they were there the whole night
But still all together they caught none
Jesus appeared and said cast to the right
And you will eventually find some

But when they realized that it was the Son
They knew they were in for a big token
One hundred and fifty-three was total sum
Even though the net wasn't broken

As you can see that the water wasn't deep
Jesus told them to come on and dine
If you really love me Peter then feed my sheep
Out of this multitude of fish I helped you find

KNOW FOR YOURSELF

After feeding four thousand on the ground
Jesus happened to look all around
People looked strange but not a sound
Was made by the disciples who stayed

What some say, Jesus didn't want to hear
He wanted to know what was in your ear
So he asked his disciples who were near
But whom do you all say

He was the one who sent to pay the price
And by his Father he was enticed
So Peter answered "Thou art the Christ"
The confession made the day

Jesus said to him "Blessed are you"
And I say "Thou art Peter, too"
Build my church on this rock, I will do
And hell shall not get in the way

WHO IS GOD?

God is the one who made this world
And everything therein
He is the one who sent his Son
To die for all our sins

He is the one who sends the rain
The lightning and thunder
He made the trees green as ever
Making them a wonder

He's the one who raises you up
And heals you from all sick
It's his time when you rise up
And not when the clock ticks

He's the one who feeds your body
Gives water when you thirst
Every good thing comes from our Lord
That's why we put him first

He's the one who answers all prayers
Treats everyone the same
Everyone should know by now
Jehovah is his name.

LET'S WORSHIP

To worship the Lord our Savior
It doesn't take a crowd
Just do yourself a big favor
And end up being proud

Serve the Lord deep from your heart
And he will surely bless you
And always take some kind of part
Do what the Lord wants you to

Not only at church but on streets
Even at the County Fair
Upon mountains, down in creeks
Worship him everywhere

We owed it to him since he came
Here filled with righteousness
If two are gathered in his name
He's right there in the midst

If you are alone out far
Not even near a phone booth
Remember wherever you are
Worship in spirit and truth

THE GREAT FLOOD

Noah warned the people that the flood would be
So he built an ark just near the sea
It rained for a total of forty days
Every now and then the water would raise

Everything in the world was destroyed
But a new world was made by the same Lord
That today we are truly living in
The same where his Son died for our sins

The people were doing everything to escape
But looks as though it was going to be late
The water happened to be drawing near
Meaning this was to be the last year

Only Noah and his family made rescue
And all of the animals were saved, too
There happened to be lots of blood
By all the people who died in the flood

CALL GOD FOR HELP

When you're in pain and feel very sore
And you need to call for help
You go right straight to the front door
God is there on your front step

All these many years he has kept
Us when we were happy or wept
Free from many sins God has swept
God is there on your front step

His only Son lives inside of us
All of us have truly felt
That's why all of us should know
God is there on your front step

You can call him anytime of day
I promise he'll be on his way
He'll answer anytime you pray
God is there on your front step

WOMAN IN ADULTERY

Jesus went to the Mount of Olives
Early in the morning and bought
All of a sudden the Pharisees
And the scribes a woman had brought

Unto him who was in adultery
Who was caught in the very act
So they brought her quickly to Jesus
Trying to prove a fact

Back in the Old Testament days
A person of such should be stoned
But Jesus came to change these things
And to these men this was not known

Jesus gave the one without sin
A good chance to cast the first stone
Immediately they all disappeared
By leaving out one by one

Next thing you know the woman was left
With Jesus all alone
That's because the scribes and Pharisees
Who all accused her had gone

JESUS CARES AND KEEPS

I'm here to let you know you'll always receive
A blessing from the good Lord if you believe
You must believe one hundred percent of his word
Of everything that the Lord has to be heard

Matters how folks treat you, you must always love
Everyone to receive the blessings from above
Even though the Lord will always love you, too
Cause he made the world, and he also made you

That's why to everyone we are to do good
And treat each other and everyone the way we should
If anyone mistreats you, leave it to the Lord
He'll settle the problem and it won't be hard

You can't just only get on your knees and pray
You also must trust and let God have his way
You'll make no mistake by saying your choice is mine
And God will keep you like he kept the true vine

TRUST IN GOD

When things aren't truly going your way
And looks like you won't make the day
And you don't have in mind what to say
Don't take life as being hard

Things will change as the time goes by
Will get better before you die
And go to heaven up on high
To receive your greatest reward

All of us have troubles and pain
Even when you're in the correct lane
All could be healed in Jesus name
If we only trust in the Lord

About the Author

Dwight Eric Conway was born in Dallas Texas on August 2, 1952. He finished high school at James Madison High and attended El Centro Community College in Dallas. Dwight has done extensive traveling to major cities in the United States as well as countries abroad, including England, France, Germany and the Holy Land.

When Dwight was a young man, he purchased a home in Dallas. Several of his church members gave financial contributions to help with the purchase. He was so well pleased and appreciative of these kind favors that he was inspired to write a poem about them. The members were so elated, that he decided to put his thoughts in writing whenever a subject came to mind. He began jotting down ideas he conceived on the streets, on the bus, at work or wherever he was. This is what started him writing poetry. Eighty percent of his poems are true. They are about people, places and things as seen from his perspective.